In My Girlfriend Voice

Deirdre K. Suggs

In My Girlfriend Voice

Published by Deirdre K. Suggs

deesuggsenterprises@gmail.com

$\mathcal{D}$EDICATION

$\mathcal{T}$o My Husband and Kingdom laborer, John the Beloved, who for over thirty-five years has watched my process in becoming what Father God desires for me to be. Your encouragement and consistent love over any matter have been truly cherished. I truly love you.

$\mathcal{T}$o My Mom Betty C. Lewis, who always exposed me to the Art of Gracious Living through entertaining in our home. You and Dad allowed us to experience the fine dining at the Millionaires Club at 19 S. Wabash in downtown Chicago, Illinois, owned by Chris C. Carson. This exclusive club was famous for its "kiddie cocktails". I thank you for always allowing me to touch your Fine China, special treasures and memorabilia in our Pecan Wood Americana Italian Breakfront which is to say "China Cabinet".

To My Godmother, Beverley Williams, who was creative enough to give me the opportunity to make $2.00 every Saturday to do light housekeeping with her, to fund my dreams. Thank you for the countless school breaks when you would take me to The Chicago Merchandise Mart and The Chicago Apparel Mart where I learned about "The World of Wholesale"

All MY Amazing DAUGHTERS In the Faith

I am so grateful To my spiritual daughter who re-lite an eternal passion back in me to see God's ladies turn into "Bride2Be Queens! Our weekly phone conference call to our first Women Submitted to the Word Shut In in January 2011 to now what has become an orchard of fruitful fruit! What a journey! Glory To The Most High God! Kingdom!!!

All MY A TEAM

To My amazing six adult children (Alex, Andrew, Angie, Ashley Aurburney, Aliyiah) who allowed "Mommie" and your dad to make many mistakes as we all learn together how to navigate life. They say that marriage and children don't come with a manual so I guess I need to write one. I pray that the many awkward situations we found ourselves in will be remembered most for the "fun" we had once we redirected our opinions of those situations.

Turning no light into going camping in the house. Having certain utilities interrupted as an opportunity to go on a mini-vacation at the nearest Four Star Hotel with an indoor swimming pool. I think of the many birthdays that were not hallmarked birthdays, but always knowing we were going to at least get a cupcake and a candle to celebrate our birth. It didn't take much and you all seemed to learn how to make good out of what others considered tragic or sad. Your perseverance and willingness to stay as a close-knit unit as brothers and sisters have inspired me to finish the many books I began to journal and write many years ago.

In My Girlfriend Voice

Bride 2 Be

"Crown For A King"

Bridal Creed

When I was a *girlfriend* I thought as a *girlfriend*, I behaved as a *girlfriend* but now that I am older, wiser and mature I pull away foolish thoughts and behavior, and embrace whole-hardly the voice of my true self!

In My Bride 2 Be Wife Voice

Bride 2 Be

"Crown For A King"

Bridal Confession

We must first take note and confess this as our profession of faith: that I am a "Speaking *Spirit*", made in the perfect image of God the Father, Son, and Holy Spirit.

I live in a *body* made of flesh from the dust of the ground formed by the hands of Almighty God: Designed as an original, fearfully and wonderfully made.

I received the Zoe breath of God in my nostrils as I became a living, thinking, independent *Soul*, with a remarkable hard drive to speak into existence the will and I am of God for my life as directed by God for God.

I am a *daughter* of God, a child of God to rule and reign and have dominion in the earth as I know it today;

I am a Royal Priesthood, with Queen status as a joint heir with Christ Jesus, seated in Him in heavenly places; given authority to tread over all the powers of the enemy and spiritual wickedness in high places.

Therefore, God knows the plans He has for me and they are good and bring me to an expected end "goal" and the mark of the high calling in Him.

God takes pleasure in my prosperity as my soul prospers; by me casting down thoughts that try to exalt itself above the knowledge of God and bring all my thoughts into captivity and under subjection to the will of God for my life in Christ Jesus.

Therefore, it is the will of God to give me the desires of my heart, for it is His word which declares that Marriage is honorable and the bed is undefiled.

For it is His word that says it is not good that I nor man be all one and alone, as He prepares me to be a suitable helmet designed to have dunamis dominion together with my husband, as the two who walks together in agreement with the Word of God which cannot return unto Him void but will accomplish what He has sent it out to accomplish.

Knowing this, that Jesus Christ will be our soon coming KING to receive His Bride 2 Be without spot or wrinkle to be caught up to the marriage feast of the Lamb. This I know and am most assured of.

In My Bride 2 Be Wife Voice

Introduction

In "My Girlfriend Voice" the book endeavors to assist ladies in exposing the subtle yet destructive hidden voice of their carnal flesh. What we say is not always what we are "saying". Women imply statements that men often interpret differently. We will begin the journey to recognize your true voice and being taught the language of a Bride 2 Be Wife.

This book serves as a type of informational and instructional guide for ladies who may not have been exposed to their "Rites of Passage" from a mother and or Titus 2 relationships.

It is a kind of look at how women should examine their own words and actions, to make the necessary changes to accomplish the end goal called *Marriage*.

Concept 1

Why Titus 2 Relationships

Titus 2 relationships are a crucial aspect for ladies who are desiring to be a wife one day. Titus 2 is a biblical expression of the rites of passage given from the older women of wisdom to the younger unmarried women.

In the thirty-first book of Proverbs, it is the Queen mother who advises her King Son Lemuel as to the characteristics he should find in the wife of his youth. She begins to instruct him and highlights her value and her worth as a wife. We often hear these passages at women's conferences as we are only getting a glimpse of what every Queen Mom desires for her King Son.

Kings today are recognized as the businessmen who have oversight of this world's goods.The word of God explains that we are to be priests and Kings, having dominion in the earth and the spirit. As you prepare to be a "Bride 2 Be Wife" and a royal diadem Crown of Glory to a King -Husband, you will begin to develop a distinct sound and that sound will be the Voice of a "Wife" and no more *Girlfriend*.

Concept 2

WiFi Revealed

When a man encounters a woman with this distinction in her voice, it is recognizable to even by the unconscious spiritually "sleeping" husband. This spirit husband which is lying dormant in the inner parts of this male "mankind" is awakened by the distinct sound of the true ribbed called "*Wife*". I like to refer to her as WiFi'

Even the untrained ear of most males can pick up the frequency of a woman who has embraced her true value and her true voice.

There is an instinctive part of a male that bows down when he is in the presence of a real lady, wife status, Proverb 14 Wise Woman & Proverb 31

..."Queen Status". A Lady who knows who she is and what value she brings as an offer to a Priestly-King awaiting his favor will stand out as a brilliant diamond among rubies and pearls.

Proverbs 12:4

A virtuous woman is

a crown

to her husband:

Concept 3

Girlfriend Voice

Well, in the pages that will follow it is my desire to help you hear yourself and identify what "Girlfriend" language sounds like and if you have been fluently speaking in that unfruitful language.

I pray you will be able to quiet and silence your spirit to begin to accurately hear the voice of your flesh. Often, I hear women in their girlfriend's voice screaming this prayer load from the Girlfriend Voice!

"GOD!
I WANT TO BE MARRIED!!!!!!
I want to just be loved! I want to
have someone to hold me! I want
companionship! I WANT TO HAVE
SEX!!! Did I forget to say I WANT TO
HAVE SEX!" Thank you kindly,
"In My Girlfriend Voice"

Uncovering The Language of
The Girlfriend Voice

Ladies, Have you ever heard the "Girlfriend Voice"? Are you familiar with "Girlfriend Voice"? Have you ever spoken in the language of the "Girlfriend voice"? This chick is so really real and her expressions outweigh the hidden treasures of the spirit wife when not put in check.

When we think about it she has had the greatest speaking practice over the years of our lives. You may ask how do we begin to hear the language of my "girlfriend" voice and how do we recognize the damage that voice has caused.

This voice is self-sabotaging in many relationships that could be potential spouses. This voice operates from a place of self-preservation, damaged emotions, and wounded spirits. Although this may be news to you it is said there is no new thing under the sun.

It is an unconscious language that has been given a voice and encouraged to be repeated since the beginning of time. This subtle yet forceful voice has always been among us. Whispering untruths, deceptions, and lies.

It was the cunning voice of the enemy in the garden which was able to input the seed of deception into the soul of the woman. The spoken seed decisively divided the soulish woman from her spirit female, stripping her from her authority and crowning value to all mankind.

Why Men Don't Take "You" Serious

From one generation to the next, it is the voice of compromise and settling for less than God's best for you. It is the voice that has been subtly handed down by women who are bewitched by fears rooted in insecurities and their sabotaging behavior. To add insult to injury we clone statements and quotes and old wives tales that empower this voice.

Have you ever heard sayings or proverbial quotes such as these?

"boys will be boys"
"he's just being a man"
" The things men do"
"It's a man's world"

Why is it when we are referring to adult males we imply in our "girlfriend voice" that their maturity does not matter? Why do we give these hall passes to aged males who display boyish mindsets? We make references to their boyish behavior and rule out their ability to exercise in a mature manner?

Why do we rule out their ability to be responsible at first sight? Why are we unwilling to challenge them to become their best self as mature men of valor?

We repeat and accept these norms and wonder why we get abnormal responses both verbally in conversation and in deeds done in our interaction with them as males.

When we look at these patterns we unconsciously engage in, we must know that they have been barriers for successfully getting to the end goal called marriage.

We must then begin to correct our own behavior as women and be intentional about the desired results. By making these efforts of changing the language of this girlfriend's voice, we then change our destination.

Remember according to the scriptures We have what we say and So as mankind, thinketh so is he or she. When we know better we do better. If we want a different outcome we have to do something different.

This book endeavors to assist you in beginning the journey to recognize your true voice and be taught the language of Bride 2 Be Wife.

Let's distinguish the difference between aged and mature. We speak of men who have aged out of puberty and their teenage years.

Just as we mentioned before these sayings like boys will be boys. We are verbally branding our males by subconsciously speaking over their lives and setting a course for them that can get ingrained in their unconscious mind. Males begin to have a belief system that they are exempt from growing up and maturing according to life charts of ...

Parents must stop giving credence to these double standards and then wonder where they developed these behaviors. This acceptance of improper behavior and adds to males adoption of the girlfriend

I would equate this thought pattern by the example of spoiled milk to buttermilk for homemade biscuits. Or rotten berries to fermented berries, which produces fine wine. Although both have gone through the process of time the outcome is not useful. It just refers to the process, aged but not beneficial.

The Indecisive - GF Voice

Let me give you some examples of the "girlfriend voice" and what she will say and not really mean, but still in hopes of a different result.

> GF ...She says " You can come by my home. If you want to!"

First of all, this part of this compound statement is really a problem. It is first rooted in a form of *manipulation* by saying "You Can"... which indicates giving options when you know in your heart you want him to visit. This form of manipulation can easily backfire on your "girlfriend" voice when "boyfriend" recognizes you have just unknowingly authorized him to have options and impromptu time frames to come as he please.

B2B will just say what she means and put it out there in plain view.

Instead of giving options, you would do better at giving a directive and being decisive.

Examples of a B2B would be...

> "Come by my home at 12 o'clock for lunch".

This statement sends a clear message to a man that you are able to make clear decisive directives regarding time, place and atmosphere. This leaves no room for misunderstanding and no open doors for lingering rejection.

Lingering rejection is defined in this scenario by potentially not getting a clear answer if he will show up or not. By not knowing the time or date, leaves too much freedom for him to have impromptu visits.

Open-ended "IF" statements should not be left on the table which is a strong indicator that response at a later time will be ok and acceptable to you. The "if" statement is also entitlement for males to think about it. Which allows time and space on his part to evaluate you. NOT good!Time and space to think on it is clearly an opportunity for him to uncover the "girlfriends" insecurities and thirsty nature that may be lying dormant in you.

And not being assured that he even "*wants*" to come by your home. Too many *what if's* are always going to be echoed by the *voice of "girlfriend"*.

It also is an indicator to a male that you have already accepted and anticipate being rejected by saying "If you want to"

Often these compound statements say one thing and then express a different outcome.

Here is another example. A female is asked where she would like to go to dinner.

She replies in her "Girlfriend Voice' … "I don't know, you decide. It does not matter, wherever you would like to go"

What happens next is usually the situation with many new dating relationships. The male decides to go to a place of his choosing and the female is not comfortable with the accommodations you become argumentative and combative. Instead of telling the truth when we ask,

"Where would you like to go?" and your reply is "It doesn't matter"
This response will show indecisiveness on your part and show manipulation and that a possible high-conflict personality existed.

Your true self usually speaks out of term, then you try to fix what you have already said and really meant. You make statements like,

    "I'm not confrontational" but you find yourself always in conflict asking yourself "why do I always say that about myself and then say "this is not who I really am". But truth be told you really are "That chick - That girl"!

The Deceptive - GF Voice

The art of deception is not acceptable. THAT IS TO SAY, "NO" does not mean no to you. Your "NO" means "Boy! Asking me another way or in another tone or in another voice". Your lack of confidence is showcased in the sound of your "No" which communicates options. When you realize you're really not saying "NO" when you say "NO" you will abandon the "girlfriend voice". You have to ask yourself "Is that who you really are? What you say you are really not saying.

For example, use of these terms, "I'm just saying" "I'm just kidding", just to be wounded by the conflict you create when "boyfriend" accepts those words as your truth.

"You know what I mean" but the 'Boy' in the friend hears you saying …" this" and you want him to know "that". What you are meaning instead of what you are actually saying to him is ineffective.

Trying to understand empty words becomes the problem for the man whose hearing what you're saying. Your words do not hold any weight because you are not true to what you are saying. You're making a lot of implied statements but not really meaning what you saying. Often this voice leads and often this indirect voice leaves the listener confused and still unaware of what you are really saying.

The Caddy - GF Voice

Sometimes females use "caddy words" or even sarcasm to express a point instead of just being very clear and to the point.

The use of sarcasm as a way to politely defend ourselves becomes a problem and often is interpreted as argumentative. Instead of politely revealing truth which I would say is a direct way of communication leaving no misunderstanding. Many females associate being truthful with becoming vulnerable, uncovered and open for "game". Often this is true when dealing with a boy and not a man sent by God.

The Manipulative - GF Voice

When you understand misplaced power becomes manipulation. A smooth voice can indicate a misogynistic background. This voice tranquilizes or puts someone in a delusional state often backfiring on the speaker. The trap set for another is often discovered or revealed leaving the manipulator abandoned and untrustworthy.

The Real Voice -Purest You

It is very important to have your own voice. Having your own voice is just like having an active say in the affairs and conversations that you are engaged in. Using your own voice gives you the power and authority to make influential decisions. You already know you do not want to constantly operate in the "girlfriend voice" because often she is perceived as your representative and not the real you. Using someone else's voice ei. The "girlfriend voice" can often cause a relationship to be sabotaged. Seek to find your inner voice. The one with the confidence of all heaven backing you up. Your words from your true self speak volumes about who you are, And to discover her is liberating and empowering. That is the "Purest You" waiting to be embraced by an authentic relationship.

We will continue in our next volume...

ABOUT THE
AUTHOR

About the Author

Deirdre K Suggs is a native of Chicago, Illinois. Raised on the south side in the heart of a historically affluent ethnic community called West Chesterfield. Raised by two professional parents. The Arts, Music and the World of Entertainment were key factors growing up and would later give way to opportunities in Print Modeling, Film and Movie exposure.

Deirdre has been selected as a print model for magazines and catalogs. Becoming a runway model paved a way for acting in feature films such as Touch and Go with Goldie Hawn and Wesley Snipes; Sixteen Candle and The Killing Floor with budding producer Bill Dukes and Whitteker. In this industry settings Deirdre would see different worlds view by her encountering various nationalities and people from all walks of life.

After her Senior year at Corliss High School. She attended Northern Illinois University and enjoyed the experience of attending Spelman College, a Historical Black College in her Junior year. It was there in off-campus housing with five amazing women from different parts of the United States that Deirdre would really experience the theme of this book. Many days the so-called "Ladies" of the house would be challenged by saying one thing and doing another. It would be weeks of seeing this inner turmoil that Deirdre

$\mathcal{D}$eirdre K Suggs has been married for over 30 plus years to Senior Pastor John Suggs and serves alongside him as First lady to Carpenter House Ministries. Inc. Together they are the parents of six children, three married to wonderful spouses, grandparents to nine and counting.

$\mathcal{D}$eirdre has been licensed and certified as an educator and clergy. Her multi entrepreneurial businesses has allowed her to service A-List clientele and prestigious organizations. Deirdre is the recipient of many accolades, awards, but is most proud of being presented the 2016 Presidential Lifetime Achievement Award during President Obama's term in office, for her life of volunteer service to her community.

$\mathcal{D}$eirdre K Suggs is a native of Chicago, Illinois. Her love for The Arts, Music and the World of Entertainment were key factors growing up and would later give way to opportunities in Print Modeling, Film and Movie exposure. In this industry settings Deirdre would see different worlds view by her encountering various nationalities and people from all walks of life.

While attending Spelman College, a Historical Black College in 1983. It was there in off-campus housing with five roommates (and their friends) from various parts of the United States that Deirdre would really experience the theme of this book. Many days the so-called "Ladies" of the house would be challenged by saying one thing and doing another. Years later to be inspired to encourage others to find their true voice.

Deidre's motto is to ...
"*Live Life to the Fullest A*
It Overflows Into The Life Of Others"

In My Girlfriend Voice

Published by Dee Suggs Enterprise, Inc

Deirdre K. Suggs

289 Jonesboro Road Suite 240

McDonough, Georgia 30253

deesuggsenterprises@gmail.com

www.ingramcontent.com/pod-product-compliance
Lightning Source LLC
Chambersburg PA
CBHW061740250726
48657CB00002B/1019